Orisa Prayers & Poems

Inspired by Olodumare

By Keisha Efuntola Temidayo

Copyright © 2024

Keisha Efuntola Temidayo

All rights reserved.

ISBN: 9798332263958

DEDICATION

To every reader may this book assist you on your journey

Table of Contents

DEDICATION i
Acknowledgements ....
Introduction 3
Giving praise 8
Mama Olodumare 12
BABA OLODUMARE 16
Esu 21
.... 21
Esu poem 24
Ogun Osin Imale 25
Ogun poem 27
Iba Ori 28
Olokun 30
Olokun poem 33
Oya 35
Jakuta Shango 38
Shango poem 40
Ibeji 42
Ibeji poem 43
Prayers for Erinle 45
Erinle poem 47
Mama Onile Mother Earth 49
Mama Earth poem 52

Prayers to Osumare	54
Osumare poem	57
Osanyin	58
Osanyin poem	60
Ochosi	61
Poem Ochosi	63
Obalu Aye	64
Obaluaye poem	67
Yemoja	68
Yemoja poem	70
Oko	71
Oko poem	74
Obatala	75
Obatala poem	78
Osun- "Ore yeye o"	79
Osun poem	81
Osun's mirror poem	82
Orinmilla, Akoda and Aseda	84
Egbe (heavenly Family)	87
Ancestors	89
To remove misfortune	91
Peace	93
Prayer to a tree	95

......95

Prayer before meals 97

Prayer for feeding fishes 98

Prayer to the elements 100

Prayer for protection and deliverance from a very evil enemy 104

Basic items used to offer to Orisa and why it's used 108

Keisha Efuntola Temidayo 112

Orisa Prayers and Poems Inspired by Olodumare

ACKNOWLEDGEMENTS

I will firstly like to thank the source of creation, life giver, and opportunity maker Olodumare for giving me the insight on how to dig out these words that were buried within me to transfer them onto paper and express these words in different ways to reach my readers. *Thank you Olodumare*

I will like to thank my Ori my divine higher self for receiving the messages and allowing me to complete this prayer book that can be shared with all that needs it. *Thank you my Ori*

Acknowledgement to my Egbe my heavenly family that never lets me down

Thank you Egbe

To my Ancestors thank you for the love and support that you provide for me on a daily basis forever protecting me. I affirm that you will continue to be elevated. *Thank you my Ancestors*

To all the various energies that assisted me

Mother Ope Ifa my love for you is beyond measure

Significant other Dorson Welch my number one supporter

Sister Ifawunmi my ride or die what will I do without you

Brother Ian Kadoo words can't express what you mean to me

Matran Ifayemesi of Matura your guidance and wisdom knows no bounds

Iya Osuntoko Abraham my first ifa teacher I have total respect for you

Those who did my hand of ifa Araba Olatunji Somorin, Olokukemi Somorin and family thank you for every opportunity that you would have given me which helped me grow both spiritually and mentally

Those who encourage me to write this book HSM baba Awurela Fakoyade

Leader Fabrice Barker thank you both for your encouragement

Those who encourage me and assisted me to publish this book, Oloye Tayese Abiye Ayele Kumari and Baba Okikifa Falade, I am extremely grateful for that final push which got things going, I appreciate you

All who continue to cheer for me in the background Ifagunwa, Ogunyemi, Ifaloba, Ire, Oriade, Chole, Suuru, Ilion and my extended family love and light to you.

INTRODUCTION

Praying to Olodumare daily is very important. Talking to Ori, parts of the creator, the universe and nature around you is very important.

There is much need for one to understand that all in existence is part of the creator's creation. Therefore, we must live in respect for the other things in creation, even if it is a fruit and its purpose is to be eaten. Respect it because it is to nourish and fuel you or whatever you as an individual use it for - it is to assist you.

It is humbling to know as a human where we stand. We are given free will, we are so powerful, yet we cannot live without a lot of things. But these very things we need will thrive and grow without us.

Just as we eat and drink, bathe and do whatever else we do on a daily basis, we must find time to pray and to connect with parts of the divine. Showing honor to even one's physical parents is very important - they are the gods you can see, therefore you should love, respect and honor your physical, earthly parents.

In one lifetime, one may not grasp the full understanding of everything, because life is a mysterious thing. For instance, we may watch a leaf as insignificant and just sweep it away, but can you understand its structure, its creation, its reason, its healing properties, and the amount of energy that went into the creation of that one leaf? As it may have absorbed properties of each element of life to bring forward its amazing product that many take for granted, this very leaf may be lifesaving or contain properties to draw money or ward off negativity.

Being respectful does not mean you let the world take advantage of you, however, do not be puffed up with pride and ego. This behavior of respect will assist us to elevate. Remember, you were not put here to judge, unless it was assigned for you to judge. You should accept that things are created differently for the creator's reason and purpose.

You are free to explore the reasons why certain things are the way they are if you wish, by connecting with the divine to seek answers to your questions.

Being grateful is a key to success. Even today, you may not have the mansion you desire, but how many other things do you have to be grateful for? You have life, eyesight, mobility, clothes, food, health, work, family, love, and your list can go on. So let gratitude become a part of your daily routine, so it will become part of your character, and this way you always have things to be grateful for.

When in the material world, acquiring material things are of importance because you are leaving behind your legacy in the physical world. However, what you are taking with you is your character. Your character is what you are here to test, as earth is like a testing ground where tests often come, and as you pass one test, another may arise. It's just like school - there is a period for learning and then the period for testing to move to another level, and when one moves to this new level in life, it may be a little more challenging. And when you become comfortable on that new level, then the test comes to be promoted, and sadly, sometimes demoted. Hence, sometimes we see our life's events repeating itself, maybe it's because we didn't pass the test to move onto the next class. Always remember, everything you do in life is being recorded, and whatever you do will reap its rewards in the timeframe it takes for one to receive according to the creator and your chosen destiny. Live in peace and be a beacon of good character, as one of the many things life can be explained as - remember, it's a journey to the grave, we all have to leave someday, make your physical existence count for something of good value.

We all have different destinies, so our good character may vary. The destiny of a hot pepper will never be the destiny of a sweet mango, so they do not judge each other - one is spicy and loved, the other is sweet and loved. We are all different, made for different purposes. Only the real judge can accurately judge our path. If you bite what we believe to be the hottest pepper in the world, and it is sweet, we will say it is out of its good character, which is to be hot. Likewise, if we bite into a ripe mango fruit and it is salty, we will say it is out of its good character, because we expect the good character of the ripe mango is to be sweet. Therefore, we understand that we are made to execute different purposes, so our good character varies according to our path.

This prayer book is to assist persons to connect with Olodumare, self, and parts of the divine, as this may assist you on your journey. Always pray sincerely from the heart, because the one you are praying to sees you for exactly who you are, as this is the one who created you. Even when praying to an Orisa, Imale, or ancestor, always include the creator's name, as full reverence and respect are due to Olodumare. Each energy reports to Olodumare, who is the creator, therefore you must remember that these are parts of the divine, but the head is Olodumare, and all other energies report to the divine source of creation. Olodumare is everywhere because Olodumare's creations are everywhere, and even though we face challenges, there are many solutions to overcome these challenges. Everything is laying within you - it's up to you to recover it inside yourself as you awaken to the blossoming of your purpose. We give thanks to the creator.

For the creator so loves the world that Olodumare gave us the Imale, Orisa's, Ori and divine destiny so that we can find ways through the wisdom of the energy that lies in each creation.

Orisa Prayers and Poems Inspired by Olodumare

GIVING PRAISE
Iba (We pay homage)

Iba Olodumare! Grand creator and all of your creation!

Iba to my Ori my grand supporter or spirt self!

Iba to the sun!

Continue to shine and bring warmth to the world! Giving off your rays of light to us and supporting our life! Everything you touch become illuminated! And is then subject to growth and development!

Iba to the plant life! The fruits and vegetation that support all life!

Iba to the animal life! The friendly and not so friendly animals that sometimes shed your blood so that we can live!

Iba to waters a gift from the havens! Both the fresh and the salt, for sustaining life, for cleansing and growing the contents of the world!

Iba to the winds of the earth! Iba to the winds of the universe! For the breath of life! The winds of positive change!

Iba to fire that brings purity, light and peace! The flame that ignites and keeps life fueled!

Iba, to the east! Iba to the west! Iba to the north! Iba

to the south! Iba heaven! Iba earth! Iba to each cardinal point! From where my blessings come from, or where I go to freely and abundantly receive!

Iba to the fowl of the air and the animals of the land!

Iba to the majestic creatures of the waters! The Underground life forms! The crickets and bees!

The flowers and trees! The herbs and barks!

Iba to those who walked before us our divine ancestors who left behind the amazing things we use from electricity to technology! To methods of healing and retrieving, to preserving, to learning, to the traditions we carry on today, and even planting seeds and trees yesterday, so that we may sit in the shade today!

Iba to this body of mines! Iba to my head,☐ my feet, my brain, my heart, my lungs, my kidney, my hands, my eyes, my ears, my tongue, my nose, my liver, my blood my bones!

Iba my bodies systems! My nervous system, my circulatory system, my skeletal system, my digestive system, my reproductive system, my respiratory system, my endocrine system, chakra system! Every cell that makes me continue to support me to have a long healthy life!

Iba to the day of my conception!

Iba to my Egbe my heavenly friends and family that always supports me!

Iba to my parents, both my carnal and my spiritual parents Iba!

Iba to this day that I am in the physical form!

Iba to wisdom! Iba to knowledge! Iba to understanding!

Iba to wealth and Aje!

Iba to the society of wise women!

Iba IFA!

Iba to all Elders!

Iba to all Orisa!

Iba to all supportive ancestors! Iba to all creators!

Iba to Odu! Iba to the universe and universal law!

Iba to my gifts and talents!

Iba to those on the left, Iba to those on the right, Iba to those above, Iba to those below!

Iba to wealth and financial freedom!

Iba to the owners of the day! Iba to the owners of the night!

Iba to the moon that brings coolness as you illuminate the night's sky and brings blessings with each cycle!

Iba to the owner of the spiritual realm! Iba to the owner of the physical realm!

Iba to my memory my memory will always be my companion!

Iba to all who taught me in my life!

Iba to the planets that supports earth!

Iba to my destiny!

Iba Orinmilla, Iba Akoda, Iba Aseda, Iba ma Osun who saved the world!

Iba to all Imale! I say Iba to all as I request the support of all Imale!

I request the support of all Orisa!

I request the support of my destiny and all the divine creations!

As I take my place in the world, universe support me in all my endeavors!

I am always blessed with peace, love, victory, prosperity, success, good health and positive wealth!

With this Iba I receive all good fortune!

Ase Ori!

Ase Olodumare!

Keisha Efuntola Temidayo

MAMA OLODUMARE

Her majesty Olodumare!

Womb of creation! From where the existence of existence comes from! From where darkness emerges light!

From where miracle and mysteries are a way of everyday life!

Our hope for era passed, our hope for era's to come!

The one who so perfectly design life, for all animate and inanimate things!

The structure for success!

The creator!

The destroyer!

The judge and the jury!

Everlasting flame!

We give you praise! We give the elements that sustain our very existence praise!

Your majestic ways surpass all that exists!

You give us free will, even after creating us, there is none like you!

How breathtaking it is to approach your throne of inexhaustible kindness.

Mother of mothers, you are not just the essence, you are the source of everything above and below the sun!

I greet the power of the goddess Olodumare shower us with your unconditional love!

Thank you for making so many things that are beautiful!

Thanks for the bitter so we can appreciate the sweet!

Thanks for the darkness so we can appreciate light!

Thanks for the pain so we can appreciate joy!

Thanks for the failure so we can appreciate success!

Thanks for the universe and all of its mysteries, so that as we unfold them, we may get to know you a little more every day!

Thanks for never allowing us to go without basic necessities!

Thanks for continuously giving greatness to us so we can share with others!

Owner of the most magnificent crown! Queen of the womb and your countless wonders!

Elevating us in whichever form we exists!

Keep us close to your heart, teach us how to overcome all that is blocking us or causing us to stumble! Give us the Ase to do your works!

Enlighten us with your uplifting spirits!

Show us how to use our gifts and talents!

The strength of the feminine energy we call on you to make us positively unstoppable!

Cleanse us from negative taught and deeds, we pour water as a payment for our deeds done in any life existence, in this life in the pass life or even in the life to come. Please use this water to replenish and wipe away the mistakes! Cleanse me of any mistakes I make knowingly or unknowingly!

Nurture us as a mother cares for her first born!

Bless us with the authority!

Bless us with abundance of good things

Good health! Wisdom! Knowledge! Understanding! And application!

Teach us how to use our gifts to make the world a better place!

Mother Olodumare I call on my Ori to receive all that you have for my growth and development! We ask not to be faced with your wrath, but to be remembered in receiving your unconditional love! Great mother of all existence! The reason for all of the magnificent wonders of our world!

Your words manifest all that is! Your love has created so many pleasures in life!

I just want to say thank you to you beautiful majestic merciful mother goddess! Your beauty and love can be seen in each of your creation! I ask for forgiveness for when I fall short of good character! Mother build me up in faith and strength! Mother bless the speech from my mouth, let me speak good things!

Bless my eyesight! Bless my ears mama! Bless my nose today! Bless my feet to take me to good places!

Bless my Ori to be the best that I can be!

Mother free me from bondage! Mother assist me to discover the gifts that is hidden inside of me! Mother send support and comfort for me! Fresh courage to go true my earthly experiences! Awaken my consciousness my mother of life! Help our people to unite! To love and shear and care for each other! Feed the hunger of my soul! Equip me to be ready to face any problem, arm me with the solution! Assist me to live in love and harmony! Let us have spiritual wisdom knowledge and understanding! Let me find the right things as I seek! Let mankind build each other up and not tear each other down! Help us to walk in accordance with the law of nature to appease your heart! Assist my bloodline to prosper if they are of pleasing character a call for assistance for them!

Beautiful, forgiving, understanding, generous, supportive, merciful, perfect, everlasting, mysterious queen words cannot truly express the magnificent meaning of your energy, may you continue to bless, protect, guide and give your resources to us. Total gratitude mother we are grateful! Mother we are grateful! Mother we are grateful!

Ase Olodumare! Ase Olodumare! Ase Olodumare!

Keisha Efuntola Temidayo

BABA OLODUMARE

Olodumare hear my call father of fathers, savior and lover of my soul, lord of my battles I place all my fears in your care!

Thanking you for the breath of life, and my existence in this physical form in this time and space!

Almighty shield and protector! Spirit of pure light! The one who deserves all worship!

Words cannot describe your magnificence!

Your majesty continue to shield our front and our backs!

Our above and below! Our left and our right!

Continue to be our blanket, cover and hide us from the eyes and acts of the wicked!

You are the creator and the destroyer, the owner of all things!

Owner of the keys to the earth!

Fearless and endless one who cannot be measured you are vast over the whole universe!

The possessor of countless blessings, mighty protector

always making ways for your faithful children!

The key that unlocks the secret of the earth, haven and the universe! You are the door! You are the key! You are the inner chamber! The way in, the way out, surely the only way!

Supreme beginning and the end! Secrets of heaven, secret of the earth!

Ruler of creation! Chief of mankind! Invincible holder of destiny!

The all sufficient one! The one who heals! The one who provides! The perfect one!

The provider! The peace maker! The judge and the jury!

The omnipotent! The omnipresent! Merciful one! Holder of wisdom of all things!

Ever faithful! Ever sure! My graceful comforter! My chief cornerstone!

The author of life! The bright morning star! My deliverer!

The one who cannot lie! Fountain of the living waters! My head! My helper!

Word of truth! Master of everything! Our guide! The breaker of curses!

The lifter of my head! The one who ensures my victory! The one who overcomes and make me to be called the overcomer!

The rock in the weary land! The shade in the parched

land!

The incorruptible everlasting light! Tower of strength who shines light in the darkness!

Maker of the Imale who sustains life!

The maker of the earth, wind, fire, water, and spirit!

The powerful sun! The he majestic waters! The ever bearing fruits and animals! The oxygen the beautiful stars!

The helper of the universe! The one who holds the answers to every secret! The word! My Shepard! My refuge! My fortress!

My light! My strength! Eyes who sees all! The great physician! My superior Olodumare I call on you oh divine light, hear me when I call on you, your child of the moment arise and reveal thy love unto me!

Be my compass and direct me!

Connect with me through your many avenues, elevate me, protect me, and reveal my own self unto me!

Give me access to my many gifts you have given me, save me from disaster! Heal me from illness! Bless me with positive abundance! Secure the health of me and my family!

Cleanse us and make us worthy of your grace and mercy!

Direct our footsteps to blessings of greatness! Connect with us in the heat of the day or in the coolness of the night!

Protect us oh god, send forward your angels, your workers, your Orisa, your Imale to save us! Forgive us for falling short of your standards. Bless our efforts!

Continue to assign our ancestors to assist and protect us! Assign your Orisa to protect us! Let the light of the day and the darkness of the night work in our favor! Reveal our purpose onto us! Don't allow the wicked to take advantage over us!

Olodumare I praise your name, I thank you also for all those that I know associate with me from your kingdom.

Iba Olodumare, Olorun, Olifi, Orisa, Egbe, Ori, Devine ancestors, Esu, Ogun, Oshosi, Onile, Yemoja, Olokun, Earile, Oya, Shango, Ibeji, Osun, Osanyin, Obaluaye, Aje, Iya mi, Baba mi, Osumare, Oko, Obatala all the Imale all Orisa I say Iba.

I bless the Odu's you gave to guide mankind! May Odu always bless me! I give praise to all Imale who sustains life!

Praise be to almighty source of life and all of your blessings! You created all things to form balance, you own the light and you own the darkness! There is nothing that can exist without your permission!

Thanks for the humans that you put in my path! Those who teach me lessons and those who assist me on my journey!

Thank you for the trials and the tribulations which has made the product you see before you! Thank you for the strength that I have been blessed with! Thank you for this body of mine blessed with all its senses! Eye sight, smell, taste, touch, hearing, my third eye, all my bodies organs, revitalize them oh god to give me sustenance to go on! Heal my organs bring them to full working potential! My heart, lungs, kidneys, reproductive system, digestive system, circulatory system mighty healer come and heal my body and even my aura, come and bless and elevate!

Always provide us with our needs and give us our wants! Merciful father give onto us the positive things that you have been keeping safe for us! We thank you for everything, you are worthy to be praised! We love you Olodumare that has forever existed and who will always exist! Deliver us from any trap or wickedness, send your searchers to check every curse, misfortune or disaster assigned to our names and destroy the possibility of it happening! In the name of the divine messenger Esu!

Ase Olodumre! Ase Olodumare! Ase Olodumare!

ESU

Iba Esu! Divine messenger, the great mediator I salute you!
Firstly, thank you for your service to God, and I am affirming that you will continue to work in my favor.
Esu does not trick or deceive me!
If you Esu must trick and deceive baba do it to those who are my enemies!
Baba Esu you are the one with the key to every door!
Baba is at this time I request you work on my behalf and open up some doors for me that I request!
And assist me to boldly step inside and receive these blessings!
Baba Esu opens the doors to medicine to suit every complaint!
Open the door of good health!
Open the door of wisdom!
Open the door knowledge!

Open the door of understanding!
Baba Esu opens the door to success!
Open the door to happiness!
Open the door to spiritual awareness!
Open the door of peace!
Open the door to patients!
Open the door to money, financial wealth, and freedom!
The door to successful businesses and successful life!
Open baba the door to Iwa Pele, good and Nobel character!
Baba open the door for my spirit guides to communicate with me!
Open the door that gives me an avenue to assist myself and assist others!
Open the door to my successful life, take me by the hand and run with me to success!
Baba Esu shoe my feet, clothe me, feed me, and keep me safe!
Baba Esu I asked you to open certain doors in my path and now I am affirming you will close some doors from affecting my path!
Close the door to loss!
Close the door to sickness!
Close the door to hate and anger abuse and addiction!
Close the door to being overwhelmed!
Close the door to poverty!
Close the door to an untimely death!
Close the door to corruption!
Close the door to bitterness!
Close the door to people doing evil against me! Don't let evil enter my path!
Close the door of people putting negative things in my children's way!
Close the door of all attacks directed to me and my

loved ones!
Divine messenger takes my prayers, petitions, and offerings to the various places they need to go to bring about positive growth and development into my life!
Great magician!
Ultimate warrior!
The skillful worker you who goes anywhere because you have such authority, I salute you and I affirm your assistance today tomorrow, and forever!
Ase Olodumare! Ase Esu!

ESU POEM

I am the divine messenger of the cross roads, one who works on man's behalf,
I can go to any direction, to complete any task.
I am the enforcer of the creator's will, yet many think I am Satan.
They blame me and call me a trickster, when they reap the fruits from their plantation.
The one who ensures you reap what you sew, and could take what you give,
Your life will be so fruitful, if only you knew how to live.
Look inside yourself this is where both good and bad dwell,
Inside you bring out your heaven, or inside you bring out your hell.
Your life is in your hands the man of the crossroad is here to guide,
It's you that decides your journey, so do you want a smooth or a bumpy ride!

OGUN OSIN IMALE

Ogun the clearer of the pathway!

Where can one reach without you? As your brother Esu open the doors, baba it is you to clear the pathway to ensure no obstacle can stop me!

Baba Ogun you who prefer to bathe in blood even when there is water at your home, do not bathe in my blood!

You the owner of metal do not let your metal harm us Ogun! Do not let your metal harm us Ogun! Baba do not let your metal harm us!

Stand on guard and search all those who enter my compound!

Ogun remove what is not good before it gets a chance to bring disgrace!

Owner of technology the strategic one, assist me to win all my battles!

Give me strength to face my trials, owner of Ire owner of blessings. Bless me!

Defend me! Uplift me! Teach me! Guide me! Protect my loved ones!

Ogun ah lakaye Osin Imole the first Imale to come to aye (earth)

Ogun you are a bringer if wealth!

A bringer of victory!

Baba bring these things to me!

Ogun your blade is so sharp there is no need to cut more than once!

I request your protection and sharpness!

Look over me and my loved ones so that harm will not come to us!

Guard us against any wickedness!

Ogun look over us as we travel on the roadways, or on the airways on the waterways and ensure our safety that we will not be victims of accidents or incidents!

You are always victorious, give us the key to success and victory!

Owner of many houses in heaven, give me a beautiful comfortable home of my own on earth!

Owner of metal give me a good vehicle to take me to and from my destination!

Protect our homes and businesses!

Take care of me and bless me with abundance, clear the way for prosperity to live with me!

Strengthen my bones as you are the owner of them! Papa Ogun when we call on you for assistance stand tall and assist your people whom Olodumare has sent you forward to assist!

Ase Olodumare! Ase Ogun!

OGUN POEM

I am the clearer of your path, by the creator rules I abide.

As you meet with many doors I clear for you to boldly step inside!

Transform iron into many useful things, from useless to full use,

And like the iron in your blood I am always with you.

Call on me a great warrior to bring you victory, this is true,

I your father is saying no enemy has any charge over you!

When you are weak use the ase of my blade to bring you power,

Because up to now there is no enemy that Ogun can't devour.

Live your life in sincerity, or else from me depart,

When giving your offerings be clean and pure in heart.

Ogun will always defend you because Ogun is the great defender

Sent to assist mankind personally by the great divine sender!

IBA ORI

My Ori is a good Ori!
My Ori I call on you!
My Ori supports me!
My Ori guides me!
My head feet hands soul body and mind is working to always be in divine alignment!
My Ori protects me!
My Ori leads me to my highest and best destiny!
My Ori leads me to prosperity!
My Ori leads me to success!
My Ori leads me to spiritual elevation!
My Ori leads me out of danger!
My Ori supports my children and my marriage!
My Ori supports Olodumare's purpose!
My Ori teaches me!
My Ori retains valuable information and ensures that I have access to it every time I need it!
My Ori accepts assistance from Olodumare and all Olodumare's divine creation.
My Ori supports me into becoming what I say I am!
I am guided by Orinmilla so I exhibit the correct behaviors that bring positive growth and development, my speech is guided by IFA I do actions that cause positive reactions in my life!
I am healthy!
I am prosperous!
I am a magnet of good fortune!
I am wise!
I am happy!
I am successful!
I am full of God's grace!

I am elevating spiritually!
I have a good physical life!
I am loved! I am respected!
I am knowledgeable!
I am understanding!
I am patients!
I am happy!
I am wealthy!
I am rich!
I am strong!
I am favored by God!
I am kind!
I am divinely aligned!
I am a blessing!
I am helpful!
I am rich and sweet like milk and honey!
I am always provided for!
I am receiving love!
I am experiencing financial growth, money flows to me in expected and unexpected ways!
I am exceeding all positive expectations! I am experiencing long life!
I am personally blessed by Olodumare, Imale, Orisa, and the energies of the universe!
I am becoming exactly who God wants me to be!
All of my life my Ori will accept the good things for me and reject anything that is meant to destroy me!
Ori I hail you! Ori I praise you! Ori I bless you! Ori bless me!
Ase Olodumare ! Ase my Ori,

OLOKUN

Iba to the ruler all bodies of water!

The one who was existing on this realm before all others!

All water bodies lead to and support you, making you vast and beautiful!

The majestic owner of the sea all waters bow down to you, all waters lead straight to you!

This is the type of support I request to have in my life's endeavors, let me too be supported by all to assist me to grow!

The beauty and riches found in your home is beyond compare!

We come to you for wisdom knowledge understanding riches and assistance in our life!

Bring healing to our vessels our bodies and our

minds!

Assist us to be patient and to How to have endurance!

Connect with us share your many positive blessings with us!

Take away all negativity with your waters!

Use your trident to bring us glory!

Defend us even if we can defend ourselves!

Olokun it is your chosen people who is calling you petitioning for a better standard of living!

To gift unto us some of your riches not only material things but also wisdom!

Olokun the body of water that can take any gender!

The one who can be raging and rough, or gentle enough to rock a baby to sleep!

The indispensable everlasting much needed Imale of the world, we invite you to bring us peace and blessings!

Show us how to use the tides and currents to bring about positive growth and development!

Water is essential for life we beg forgiveness for the pollution mankind has put into the water ways!

Our survival depends on you!

Continue to show us your unconditional love and share with us your resources!

The holder of many of our ancestors, we greet you all

in the name of Olodumare!

Praising the Imale Olokun for all that you do for us and the world!

Olokun chief of the waters always ensure our safety in your waters!

Never let water cause our destruction!

Let's water always bring me victory!

Olokun Aje let water always bring me richness!

Let water always bring me the stability and coolness!

Mysterious and everlasting Olokun bring peace and prosperity, abundance and positive blessings!

Olokun Aje the wealth of the sea, the wealth giver positively bless me today, with wealth of each positive type!

Olokun Aje you are wealth and wealth is you, your house holds so many riches and forms of life I give praise and honor to your majestic energy. May each lifeform that reside in you support me, let all water bodies support me!

Ase Olodumare!, Ase Olokun Aje.

OLOKUN POEM

Out of the deep where mystery is hidden,

But when we call on you, you come and you listen.

Known as the chief owner of all the waters,

The one who always supports your sons and your daughters.

Holder of wisdom, riches and so much more,

When one connects with Olokun, you explore mysteries that take you through different doors.

Master mermaid, master diver holder of riches beyond understanding,

As you connect with your chosen ones the knowledge just keep on expanding.

Like a shimmering and shiny pearl you illuminate a smooth waving motion in the dark,

We are protected in your waters, your magic causes us to swim like a shark.

Olokun's children are wise and opportunity always brings them wealth,

Using your trident to direct and protect us, keep us in best of health.

Olokun gets full respect from all who knows about the mystery,

The first force here even before the earth, go and check out creations history.

OYA

Iba ma Oya!

Mother of the wind, prosperity, change, the cemetery gates, the market place!

You who is always present cause wind is always there!

Oxygen helps all to survive!

Blow away the negativity from our lives and bring winds of positivity!

You are our mother!

When as a tornado even in farce violent times we will be kept safe from the storm safe and calm!

Protect us from what wants to harm us!

Defeat our enemies on our behalf!

Don't let us see the cemetery gates before our time!

Protect your children mama Oya!

Don't let us experience your wrath give your wrath to our enemies!

Those who fight against your children fight against you!

Those who fight against you fight against your husband Shango!

We respect you Oya and we respect your husband Shango!

We acknowledge your winds of life!

Don't let us be cut out from air mama!

We appreciate the breath of life and the oxygen you provide us with!

Mother make our business place busy as the market place new and old customers keep coming for the products we have to offer!

Mother pass by and take the evil that people has left behind and deliver it back to their doorsteps or take it to a place where it can no longer do no harm to us!

Do not let any of the negative things of this world harm us!

No negativity shall affect or offset us!

All that want to destroy us must face the destruction they place in our path!

All that is negative must not affect or offset us!

The winds of haven and the winds of earth all winds of Oya will protect me!

Oya support me to make positive changes, that will always bring me more prosperity and success spiritually and physically grooming me to be counted among the successful people on earth. Always let me return home with victory and positive abundance, great one that supports in Aye and Orun give me messages that will ensure my success.

Ase Olodumare!, Ase Oya!.

Oya poem /song

Mother of the wind, mother of change,

Mother who can make one's life re arrange.

The first breath is oxygen from thee,

I am grateful that you give oxygen freely to everybody.

You blow winds so gentle that makes people fall in love.

And even blow winds of destruction, with full authority from above.

Ma Oya thank you for your oxygen, and your positive winds of change,

Always blow positivity into my life and in good let me engage.

Warrior fighter fierce when she needs to be,

I call on ma Oya to always defend me. ☐

Colorful skirt of 9 colors blowing in the wind,

True protector of her husband and of her children.

Assistant of the ancestors, assistant to us in flesh,

Please blow your winds to enlighten us so that we will always be refreshed.

JAKUTA SHANGO

Iba Shango, Jackuta, Oba kuso

Praise the spirit of thunder and lightning!

The god of justice!

God of dance!

Lord of fire!

Father it is you we call upon to win our battles!

It is you who we call upon to fight all wrong doings that are being done to us!

You who have the double axe that is meant to defend us!

Take up all my battles and make me victorious!

Give me victory over known and unknown enemies!

Those that ill speak your children feels the full wrath of your thunderstones!

Shango use your thunderstones to defend us!

He that loves to dance and have a good time give us happy days in life so we can be joyous!

Give us several reasons to celebrate!

Devour our enemies, and like lightening after you strike there is no need to strike again!

Let us walk with the authority of Shango!

Let us have the power of Jahcutta!

As we face the days of life let us have justice!

Justice in our homes!

Justice in our work, and day to day activities!

Walk with us wherever we go!

Defend us in every situation show us favor!

Bless our hands!

Bless our feet!

Bless our heartbeat!

Don't let harm come near our path, be vigilant, and keep us safe!

Accept all our offerings and delight in the sight of your children!

Help us to grow wherever we are planted!

Your children are rich, your children always have food, clothes, shelter, life, victory, success, knowledge, wisdom, joy, laughter, honor, respect. We are your children let us have the things that your children have!

Ase Olodumare! Ase Jakuta Shango!

SHANGO POEM

Justice, strength, lightning and thunder,

Its baba Shango so there is no need to wonder.

The electric force zapping through the sky,

Your double headed axe is a defender that I honor with pride.

You can break evil curses injustices and spells,

Jacuta Shango ensures that his children are well.

What an energy to have close on my side,

You never leave me without you always provide.

Oba koso the one who is royal,

I place my battles in your hands for you are true and loyal.

As I keep you close to my heart,

I ask you to keep me on the right part.

One who loves the drum and dance, father full of life,

The wise powerful king who gives abundance and answers to my plight.

May the lord of justice show me favor, of good character let me be,

With Shango on my guiding path I fear no enemy.

IBEJI

Praise the spirit of the twins Iba Ibeji,

The children of the Orisa family!

Protected by all the Orisa's, may all the Orisa protect us just as the Ibeji is protected and taken care of!

Ibeji bring us abundance of joy, prosperity, wealth, happiness, and good fortune!

Bring us honor and good luck!

Double our resources!

Make every situation into a good one with your magical ase!

Bring balance and peace!

Elevate us and don't let those working against us bring us any harm to us!

Sweeten us and give us victory over known and unknown enemies!

Don't let anyone steal our blessings our gifts and our virtues!

Keep us happy and as cheerful as childish glee, just like when you receive blessings from all Orisa's let me also recieve!

Twins visit the poor to make them rich!

Twins elevate their parents!

Ibeji brings many blessings from heaven to earth!

Ibeji opens doors of prosperity, money, abundance, good luck and many blessings!

Ibeji is welcome to come and bring blessings!

We thank the spirit of the twins!

Ibeji who holds many keys, I affirm you will open doors of positive Ase that will bring about positive growth and development!

Ase Olodumare,Ase Ibeji!.

IBEJI POEM

One who Ibeji visits is one that is truly blessed,

They come to open doors of wealth, prosperity and success.

They make the poor house a house of abundance, they cover the backs of the clothes less.

Ibeji chooses the house of the poor over the rich to bring them success.

Ibeji holds the keys that will make you move from darkness to light,

Come and double my resources and make my future bright.

The spirit of the twins fill my house with laughter happiness and joy,

Wealth, prosperity, goodness and balance like girl and boy.

Come to me in the day or even in the night,

Bring to me positive growth and development, let us all delight.

PRAYERS FOR ERINLE

Iba Erinle

Praises to the multi-diversity of Orisa Erinle

Where sweet water meets salt water!

Where victory is sure!

Erinle Ajaja the skilled one in the water!

The skilled one on land!

A great healer and hunter!

One who can adapt in any situation!

The power of Erinle is as strong as the currents of the sea and can be sweet at fresh water!

Swift flowing life giving, praise to the versatile Orisa!

The farmer! The herbalist!

The fisherman!

Father help us with everything!

Strong, brave and firm Erinle come from wherever you are and listen and approve of our request and affirmations!

You are wealthy and well-dressed grant us wealth of our own so that we can also look fine!

You are a master healer and herbalist grant us good health so that our lives can be long!

You are always full of life grant us long happy life!

Clean us inside and out, give us versatility as you are so that we can never be stagnant!

Show us favor and protect us from harm, loss, tragedy, death, sickness, danger, negativity, unclean spells, wickedness, false people and all ills of the world!

Erinle give us favorable growth, development and protection!

Keep us cool, bless us in all areas of our lives!

Bless our ancestors!

Reward us for our efforts!

Assist us find comfort in life!

Protect and give us mental health and wellbeing!

Help us to be brave and fearless but wise!

Reveal the mysteries of yourself to us so we can connect with you!

Bless our homes and our paths!

Let all weapons formed against us fail and crumble and be washed away!

Let all those who are going out of their way to harm your people find no peace until they stop and turn away from their wicked acts!

Let them find the light of God so that they depart from their wicked acts and thinking and that they may repent and work on changing to good character where with this change they may find healing!

Encamp around our homes and yard and chase all negativity out!

Success and prosperity is from where you are planted up to miles away!

Keep us successful and prosperous!

Petition to your neighbors on our behalf let them too assist us in our cause let your people rise!

Let your people be happy, prosperous, protected, skilled, magnificent, healthy, wealthy, successful, have good relationships, good jobs, homes, cars, luxury, food, we are your people Erinle grant us these things and all blessings

Ase Olodumare! Ase Erinle!

ERINLE POEM

Versatility has arrived, can work well in the water or land,

Works in fresh or salt a haunter in any territory water, forest, beach or sand.

One who gives medicine, one who scares away death!

When you put your trust in him it's something you

won't regret.

Where the river meets the sea you can find mixing tides,

It takes a special type of being to go to any atmosphere and reside.

Erinle brings peace, Erinle brings wealth,

Erinle brings success, and restores your health.

When you call on a versatile master who can assist with any case,

He will not leave me defenseless, he can assist me with anything I face.

Erinle Ajaja can be ferocious as a dog,

Stand in front my enemies and defend me from their calls.

Protector and defender Ajaja Erinle

Strong courageous elephant is on my battle font so intruders be wear.

MAMA ONILE MOTHER EARTH
Iba Mama Earth

Praises to the mother of the earth!

Request and thanks to you O queen!

Mother what can one give to you that is not already yours?

You are the world we give you praise!

You sustain life of every living thing!

You nourish and fertilize all that is!

It is you that give us our bodies in so many amazing rich shades of brown!

It is you who provide our feet with solid place to walk on!

It is you who give way for grains to grow!

It is you who give animals food to provide us with milk and meat!

It is you who give the bees flowers to give us sweet

honey!

It is you who give the rivers banks so that it can contain water!

It is you who give us fruit to make wine!

It is you who take our debris and make a new earth to nourish new trees so that we can breathe!

Mother bless us!

Mother forgive us for the harm that we do onto you!

Make our lives rich and fertile as you are mother!

Help us to maintain our faith!

When we think that all is lost let there be renewed life and hope in us with new opportunities to overcome the trials that we face on a daily!

May we be victorious!

May all what our hands touch be successful!

May we walk with authority and blessings of the earth!

May our homes always be stable!

May no earthquakes affect our homes!

May no form of natural disasters affect our homes!

May there always be food in our cupboards and in our fridge!

As we feed the earth Mother you feed us!

Keep negativity off of our surroundings!

Let those who set traps for us on your grounds mother, may you swallow their trays and swallow them also and take it to a place it can do no harm to us or others!

Bless our lands to be fertile so our crops grow abundantly and bountifully!

Bless our feet as we walk on your land!

Bless our Ori's, as we bow to greet you divine Goddess of the earth!

As we honor you Mama Onlie may your seal of growth, development, abundance, wealth, health wisdom and all that is good be upon us!

Thanks for your blessings Mama!

Ase Olodumre! Ase Onile!

MAMA EARTH POEM

The earth is rich the earth is fine,

The earth is one of the main ingredient in the existence of mankind.

The earth nourishes all that is even when we as humans neglect,

So what have you done lately to show the earth your respect?

Have you littered her inconsiderably and caused an eye saw?

Or have you brought her so much harm she can't heal herself anymore?

Did you bother to say thank you to mother earth and hope she accepts your offering with faith?

Or do you only remember that she exist when there is a major earthquake.

All we see in existence on the planet earth we must treat with love,

For on this physical plane without the earth there will be no below or no above.

Get your act together mankind check through your behavior with a fine tooth comb,

Because of all of the life on this planet you are the only

ones destroying your home.

Treat mother earth as best as you can because everywhere you turn you can see her,

If this is how you treat what you can see in the physical how will you treat an unseen creator?

PRAYERS TO OSUMARE

Iba Osumare O!

Rainbow beaming your colors across the sky, only peace and calm can come to ones heart after seeing your majestic colors, arranged in a reflection of love!

You come forward to comfort us after the rain!

To bring hope!

You who turns things around!

Turn my sadness into joy!

Turn my sickness into good health!

Turn my poverty to prosperous wealth!

Turn my weakness into strength!

As I go through each cycle in life you are a reminder that beautiful things are on the way!

Steer me through my cycles to learn and grow and to positively change!

Give me the strength to master each cycle!

Open up my chakras, so I master each color and be in alignment!

To shine and to know when to show myself!

For spiritual consciousness to come and fill me so I can become the best version of myself!

Help me see the beauty in myself and even the beauty in others!

Help me to love myself and teach me to love others!

To trust myself and show me who to trust!

When Osumare comes to bless us we are truly blessed!

I give praise to the energy of Osumare!

Continue to bless your people, illuminate the sky and our life!

Illuminate my life with color!

Brighten my armor and aura!

Red! Awaken my passion and love!

Orange! Awaken my creativity, vitality, and versatility let me give and receive love!

Yellow! Make me as rich as gold and beam light of elevation from the sun!

Green! Give me wealth, growth, balance, health and fertility!

Blue! Give me good luck and courage, spiritual elevation, connection with the water!

Indigo! Give me awareness of self and the divine in me!

Violet! Let me connect with my spiritual consciousness!

Osumare bring the peace of god in your colors that you bring into our world!

Putting me in alignment awakening my kundalini, to the memory of my very being

that I who walk on the face of the earth is in a perfect array of color,

that balances who I was, who I am. and who I will become.

As the wise serpent uses its head to find its way

I will always find my way to victory.

Osumare blesses me abundantly guiding me toward my own pot of gold that brings out the best in me.

I experience the aura of the rainbow as Osumare awakens me

Ase Olodumare! Ase Osumare!

OSUMARE POEM

Aligner of the chakras colors of life unfold,
Mystery of the rainbow so much more to be told.
Brighten up the sky with colors like a crystal you shine,
Owner of the pot of gold at the rainbow, make some of your riches mine.
You assist with cycles and transformation, you show your beauty on the sky,
Teach me how to reveal my beauty, the things I learn in life let me apply.
You who awaken consciousness in the beautiful flow,
Let us be as radiant as a rainbow anywhere we go.
As we raise our vibration our colors will expand,
And the loving Osumare will ensure that as we grow we understand.

OSANYIN

Iba to the master of the herbs, the lord of the leaves, barks, flowers and roots!

You know the secret of every herb! Your Ase turns everything into a magical potion!

To heal to restore, to renew and even to devour!

Grate magician I call on you baba Osanyin, I call on you Baba Osanyin for prosperity healing longevity and your teachings!

Imale of the herbs teach me how to make sweet blends to make my life prosperous!

Teach me how to cover myself and my loved ones, so that no evil or destructive force will be able to penetrate us!

Help me to appreciate the plants and herbs, as you educate me on so many antidotes and show me how to awaken the properties of the herbs, I give you thanks for your service to not only humankind but also your support to our planet earth!

Papa Osanyin come and make medication!

Come and give medicine for good health!

Good medicine for our eyesight!

Medicine for sharp intellect, to restore our people!

Come Osanyin come and free us from depending on western medicine

Keeper of the forest your medicine is most effective!

Revitalize my body and its organs with herbs!

Continue to shear your herbs with us and the other deities who continue to bring your blessing of healing to us!

King Osanyin! Father Osanyin! Grate Osanyin!

Herb master! My defender! I praise your name bless me with your powerful Ase!

You who can hear me whisper from miles away!

You who can give medicine to suit each complain!

I call on you to build up my immune system let it function just as it was made to support long healthy life!

Let the herbs enrich my spirit!

Let the herbs support my journey!

Spirit of the herbs speak to me through your herbs reveal your secrets!

Teach me all about the money drawing herbs tell me what to do so that it will bring me financial wealth!

Teach me about the herbs for protection, herbs to get back good things that I may have lost!

The herbs to wash my Ori and to keep my Ori satisfied!

Teach me about herbs to assist barren women!

The herbs to keep the brain sharp and working and to assist with memory!

The herbs that combat any illness, the miracle cures in the correct dosage!

The herbs that support human life! Thanking you for all your assistance
Ase Olodumare! Ase Osanyin!

OSANYIN POEM

Herbalist in the word that knows every plant,
Some you can just pick and use others awaken with a chant.
Osanyin master healer we consume you every day,
Be it in our green salad green seasoning into our system you find a way.
May you always bring healing even if we consume in small quantity,
You keep us safe with herbs bringing blessings abundantly.
Show us how to use you to treat our pains,
Restorer of good health heal the blood in our veins.
Osanyin baba thank you, for you mean so much to me,
Show me how to use your flowers, show me how to use your tree.

OCHOSI

Iba to the sharp shooter!

The owner of the river banks! The one who never misses his target!

Grate hunter direct me!

Assist me so that I do not miss my targets grate hunter direct me!

Show me the way to always achieve my goals, steer my Ori to good places, good opportunities, so that I can be successful in life!

Use your bow and arrow to defend me, guard me as you guard the river banks!

Guide me as you guide your arrow to hit its target!

Strong and powerful one who is eternally blessed look over my compound! Shoot down the weapons of those that want to harm me!

Protect me and those who wish me well! Protect me from the long arm of the law and the short arm of the law! If I ever have any court case make me the victorious one!

As a hunter Baba you are a provider, always provide me with food shelter and protection!

Help me to be wise and strategic just as you are while you hunt so that I will always be victorious!

You are a bringer of swift justice, assist me in my battles, those spiritual battles that I face because of wickedness that persons against me for no reason!

Fighting me without cause and purpose baba grant me swift justice!

Grant me justice so that I can live in peace, track my enemies and bring me victory!

Show my enemies even onto the light of Olodumare so that they may turn from evil to good!

Point them to the light of god, so that they may stop doing bad and start doing good deeds! If they don't want to change from doing evil, then return their seeds of wickedness with the speed of your arrow! You are spirit so I know you will read the mind and heart of all of us and deal justly with us!

Ase Olodumare! Ase Ochosi!

POEM OCHOSI

The sharp shooter, the one blessed with the ase to never miss his target,

Hit your goals at the correct time strategize and achieve it.

The greatest haunter of all time wisdom and skill is needed on the hunt,

Always direct us on our path to achieve the desires we want.

Left handed magician of the forest we call you on our quest,

When it comes to sure direction we only call on the best!

When we call to hit our target who better for this fight,

All we have to do is call on you be it day or night.

Bless us with your bow and arrow and uplift our minds,

To remain in range of our target to execute it in the right time.

Ochosi strategic warrior hunter one who offers grate defense,

Direct all our enemies shots back to their residence!

OBALU AYE

King of the earth. Chief of healing! Whenever Obalu Aye visits me, he visits to heal, he takes away all sickness!

He removes all sadness and tragedy! Obaluaye comes to heal, to protect, to restore to uplift! He comes to remove all diseases!

The number one cure for all problems have arrived!

He will not bring us any problems!

Rather Obaluaye is here to heal all problems!

We pay homage to you! We give gratitude to you!

You who bring good health and wealth to your people!

You heal all illnesses and suffering weather it is natural or supernatural you are the cure!

Your medicine is the cure! Your herbs and powerful Ase will bring desirable results!

You will not leave me in a bad situation!

You will correct anything that is going wrong!

We affirm that we will not die in an epidemic!

We will always be protected!

Our mental health will always be well!

We will always be of sane and sound mind!

Save us from destruction, from the chemicals they put into our food, from the medication designed not to heal but to damage other organs!

From the chemical filled water that we drink, to the genetics that is modified in the food!

Let all of these still never block us from spirituality!

May they never hide us from our Gods again!

We must never be enslaved or entrapped again!

We must find healing and medication for each complain!

We affirm overall wellbeing, strength, good health and that all we consume acts as medicine to revitalize sooth and heal us!

We affirm that we be granted long healthy life, that sickness will not visit with us!

That you Obaluaye will direct us to the prevention of all illness and also to the cure!

You the commander of health restore our health!

Fix our bodies put us in good working order!

Save us Obaluaye save us from all sickness and destruction!

Tend to my bread basket today you who also brings one wealth, I affirm you bring me wealth of each positive type!

Baba sweep me with your healing broom!

Fill my hands with prosperity!

Put success in my dwelling! Full my pockets with cash money! Bless me so that I can help myself!

Continue to be the lifter of my head!

A guide showing me the way, a waterer to make my grass greener an answer to my call!

Let your mercy endure!

Let your healing power roam my premises and remove all sickness in the area and dismiss it to not return!

Ase Olodumare!

Ase Obaluaye!

OBALUAYE POEM

God of sickness and epidemics, what a powerful energy
That there is no cure he cannot find he is the natural remedy.
When Obaluaye visits it's to take away sickness,
And he leaves behind in our path success, richness and wellness.
Chief of the earth holds the secrets of all healing on earth,
When they say your health is your wealth it's the sick man that knows what health is really worth.
Obalyaye bring me good health and cures to suit each complain.
Take away all sickness and keep me sane.
Obaluaye visits me today and bring me healing and peace,
Whatever negative may be in the yard or the body let its power cease.
One who can bring sickness or take it away I am calling on you to heal,
And any time you visit me I ask that its healing you come to reveal.

YEMOJA

Mother of the fishes mother of abundance, mother who nurtures and protects, mother that is so loving that your fish feed the other animals of the world, how to rightfully praise such a deity. You along with the other Imale are truly of love!

I give u praise you have given service to our creator Olodumare and given service to mankind! You represent so much what we aspire to be! Queen Yemoja!

Fertility, richness, prosperity and wisdom continue to bless us!

A mother to run too because she is sure to help and protect her devotees!

A mother loves, a mother disciplines, a mother teaches, nurtures, loves and gives freely.

We find fishes in the fresh waters, we find fishes in the salt water you make yourself so accessible and versatile to show your love for all!

Come and embrace us, protect us, uproot domestic violence from our people!

Remove backstabbers!

Solve family problems!

Help me to love myself!

Restore peace on our land!

Mother you can understand my tears!

Mama I know you feel my pain, take me through this rough patch now as I still say praises onto the creators name!

Where I am empty full me up, when I am weary renew my faith!

When I am about to fall please raise me higher!

Yemoja the lifter of my head! You who make barren women conceive let our bloodline be fruitful!

Let our lives be full with prosperity!

You know you can also be a fierce protector, protect us from all that wants to bring us pain! Protect us from evil works and doers, let us have your spirit of abundance and love throughout our lives!

Ase Olodumare! Ase Yemoja!

Keisha Efuntola Temidayo

YEMOJA POEM

A mother of fishes, what comes to mind is abundance and life,
A giver a nurturer one whose protection can be as sharp as a knife.
One who clothe and covers, one who washes away sin,
One who stands by her children the mother of the finned.
She stands by mankind she nurtures she protects,
She feeds us she washes us to her we show honor and respect.
Mother who understands and assist, and just like the cycle of the moon,
You can help things come into fullness, or to be lose in the darkness or give a chance for a new.
Yemoja great mother who can be very calm or very rough,
We make offerings as we praise your name, may it always be enough.
You was there with mankind through slavery, now you are still here while we are free,
This is why we find it fit to always pay homage to the sea.
Great mother who saves great mother who gives,
Teach me your wisdom, show me the correct way to live.

OKO

The deity of the farm fertility and agriculture who carefully tends to the crops and makes harvesting abundant, from a tender care of a seedling to make a mature bearing plant!

Orisa Oko let our yields multiply, let our crops bear abundantly, fertilize our animals so that they multiply and bring good healthy strong animals!

Assist those of us who want children to conceive and bring fourth healthy good children!

Oko bring us financial success!

Productivity at our work, healthy crops, blessed hands, strength to go through each cycle! You the most successful farmer assist us to yield bountiful harvest each year!

You are also a healer of infectious diseases!

It is you who cures even death! God of the fields!

Restorer of fertility!

When Orisa Oko supports me I must grow!

I will grow because baba Oko supports me, Oko makes me fruitful and wealthy!

Come and support me and bless me so that I can support myself and my children!

Protect my crops from pest! Protect my life from pest, from energies who only want to feed on me and leave me drained, who only want to take and give nothing in return!

Let us always have jobs!

Let our seeds always germinate and multiply bringing bountiful harvest.

Orisa Oko come and make positive differences in my life!

Come and restore me come and elevate my life!

Come and make me grow like a tree planted by the river side, and like that tree all I need must flow to me!

Don't let my blessings pass me by, but let me have them and enjoy them in my life!

Thank you for restoring what was lost, thank you for bringing things that are new, thank you for the blessings that you just planted in my life that I will reap in some time to come!

Thank you for the wisdom, knowledge and understanding!

Strengthen me to cultivate the land. If I am just like a seed let me rise out of the ground like a young plant prune me in the way I should grow!

Make my lands fertile and ever-growing, strengthen me on every bending side!

Rejuvenate the wisdom in my DNA! Let me shine and shine my light on others, let no one pluck my beauty from me!

Reveal to me the mysteries of success have me like an ever bearing plant, never being left without but always have something to give! Bring me to enlightenment, weather it takes a short period or lengthy days assist me on my journey!

You know your importance in human life do not turn away from us, but give freely as you as you can! We receive all your blessings!

Ase Olodumare! Ase Oko

OKO POEM

Lord of the fields and plants, restorer of the land,
Ensuring bountiful harvest, supplying the worlds demands.
You keep us fed and healthy, you make seeds multiply,
Oko deity of the farms and harvest may your mercy never pass me by.
One of your gift is fertility, touch my livestock today,
So that I can have a land of plenty, in each and every way.
Let our crops be of highest grade, let us be lifeforms of success,
Let everything our hands touch, or what our Ase speaks on always come out to be the best.
Let all our surroundings and us be healthy, let our flowers bloom,
Touch our blessings with fertility, our crops our finances, our wisdom, growing to positively manifest like a baby being delivered from the womb.
Growing to adulthood let us be strong and free, well rooted foundation bearing fruits that are always blessed by thee.

OBATALA

Iba Obatala God of purity! Molder of the head! Pure supreme justice!

Protect our ori!

With this prayer father Obatala open up my ways and shine your light so that I can see my way! Lead us with your faith!

Direct and pour your blessings upon us so that we can become stronger!

Help us to vibrate in tune with our divine creator!

Free us from any traps or necromancy!

Let our light shine when necessary so that darkness does not possess us! Expose evil doers! Build us up in faith!

Remove and discard anger!

Remove sorrow and hatred from us!

Tame the heart of our enemies! Let those who wants to destroy us see the light of god, and turn away from their evil ways and turn to serving god in spirit and in truth!

Help us to develop patience baba Obatala perseverance and forgiveness!

Help us to be charitable, to have faith and hope and love for our fellow neighbors!

We receive you Obatala, lead us with your faith, and let us always find the house of Olodumare necessary, so that we will never weaken in the face of disturbances!

Allow me to have peace and happiness, and show me the path to receive the choicest gifts of god!

Make us centers that are emitting energies to combat the forces of evil that plague our planet earth!

Stand on guard baba, let us be a part of the solution to bring about the regeneration of the planet earth! Let us never have to be destroyed by greed, intolerance, and a lack of respect, hunger, and wars of any kind, a lack of faith or anything to bring about destruction!

Baba please protect and shield us, help us to live in harmony forming a single vibration of a unique sound to combat the evil wave that pervade the astral of the earth! Even if we are few Obatala don't let us stand alone!

Allow our strength to be multiplied! Multiply our strength by the mighty unity of all our protectors!

Obatala may your arms always be open to us to support us, to love us, to cleanse us, and assist us! Chief of the white cloth grant us a white cloth of our own! Save me Obatala! Obatala save us! Give us the power to manifest abundance! You who always fight for what is right! King of kings bless our generations! Help us to live in love, peace and happiness purity and prosperity!

Cover us and purify us from all stains that are causing obstacles, all that is stopping us from achieving our goals and our positive growth!

We ask for your assistance to shine your light so bright on the stains till they are cleansed!

So they can no longer hold us back!

Help us to elevate spiritually!

Father Obatala shine your light of peace and prosperity and protection on our Ori's, on our life!

We ask you to guard guide and protect us always, today and every day!

We thank you baba Obatala, we give praise and thanks to Olodumare we give praise and thanks for the support of all that is good!

If anyone is using my name for evil, I request that you purify the action cleanse me and cover me with your white cloth!

Ase Olodumare, Ase Obatala.

OBATALA POEM

One who is pure and loves white cloth, shines light and covers me,

The molder of mankind the molder of the head, to patience you have the key.

Cover me with your white cloth and hide me from danger,

Like a baby cover me with your cloth from seen and unseen danger.

The one who I can climb upon the mountain top to meet,

I bow in your presence and receive blessings at your feet.

Cotton is precious to you and so too we are precious,

When we call on you we know you always refresh us.

You support human life, you keep us in check,

Very compassionate father who corrects us you are the best.

Bring peace as you touch our Ori and revitalize our cells,

Chief of the white cloth who loves silver bells.

OSUN- "ORE YEYE O"

Goddess of love, sweetness, richness, success, self-reflection, sexuality, sensuality, romance, power, wealth, one who is as sweet as honey, arise to my call!

Healing sweet waters, restorer of joy! You who saved the world from drought and destruction! Our savior! You whose name is the same as saying unconditional love!

Mama Osun Imale come and receive my request! Thank you for your love, refresh me with your cool waters! Enrich me with success and abundance! As I tap into the essence of water, just like water I will always find my path!

I will always be victorious! I will always be of good use! I will always bring coolness and life!

Water my finances with prosperity! So that my money multiplies to see me through my intentions!

Sweeten my relationships! You are a giver of love, happiness, wealth, healing prosperity, fertility and so I affirm that you will grant me these things that you give!

Give me peace in the world and peace in my soul!

Give me confidence in myself to overcome my hurdles!

Heal me with your waters and cleanse all negativity in my path!

Shower me with love and peace! Restore my crown!

Like the river flows let all good things flow into my life! Let me blossom as you water me!

Let me have a good life here on earth! Bless my family and my children!

Just as the river is known for its sweet water, fishes, life and flowing, let me too also be known for grate things!

Let me be known for success! Let me be known for prosperity! Let me known for wisdom! Let me be known for love and gracefulness! Let me be known for good character! Let me be known for assisting persons! Let me be known for making good choices! Let me be known for taking care of my people! Let me be known for winning! Let me be known as victorious! Let me be known as the bearer of good children! Let me be known as strong and beautiful! Let me be known as anointed by the almighty! Let me be known as protected and blessed!

Let me walk with the grace and abundance of milk and honey like Osun!

Like Osun's honey let me never spoil! Let me heal and

bring smiles and joy! Mama Osun I receive your blessings and love!

Ase Olodumare! Osun!

OSUN POEM

Who is sweetness, the fragrance of love?

Its mama Osun whom all ones problems solve.

Flowing sweet waters pure grace from god,

Your mysteries so deep, man can only watch in awe.

Luscious and radiant, pure and true,

Sweet as honey we come to you.

Come to you for your love, your healing, your success,

To purify our bodies as you nurture us from your breast.

Mother who loves brass and cleanness of heart,

Your love is what the world needs put love in our path.

We all use your waters you reside in the DNA of man,

Speak to us in our bodies to execute god's plan.

You saved the world before we know you can do it again,

Please use your healing waters to remove our pain.

OSUN'S MIRROR POEM

Looking at the mirror what will you see?

A gorgeous and pretty face full of beauty.

But now look yourself in your eyes, and look at your soul,

Is it now the same beauty that you behold?

Dig deep and only then you can see what god sees,

It's your character, your behavior, and your love, leading you to life's keys?

Where is your key to success, your key to the kingdom of God?

Your key to salvation, you are creating your own life's reward!

No key to open the door to your physical senses, far more for the spiritual.

Your thankfulness to almighty god should be a daily ritual.

Look in the mirror until you can find,

The very solution to your peace of mind.

Osun grate mirror of mystery,

Is saying to you, look in the mirror what do you see?

ORINMILLA, AKODA AND ASEDA

Iba to Orinmilla, witness to creation and your first two disciples Akoda and Aseda.

Together you bring the message from the creator and from creation! You hold the wisdom of yesterday today and tomorrow!

Entrusted in your care are the secrets of creation, and the roads and paths one can take to achieve their highest and best destiny!

Orinmilla bring me success today, teach me as you teach your disciples! Let me live a good and fulfilling life a life of ever bearing good things!

Let me continue to see into yesterday today and tomorrow if this is pleasing to Olodumare!

Show me the remedy for my situation! To be victorious in my battles! Let me have good human experience!

Let me meet with friends and not with foes! Let my words be words of power! Words of wisdom! Words of truth!

Bring my blessings to me or send me to where I must collect them!

Let me have good family life! Let me have good relationship with the divine!

I call on you today to uplift my spirit! Shine your light on my destiny!

Show me who I am today and who I am meant to be!

Help me to walk in my alinement!

Show me how to use the materials provided to achieve desirable outcomes!

Activate me today!

Rise me up in faith and power! Educate me sufficiently!

Let me never be trapped by illusions! Show me truth and keep me wise!

Show me the way to gain the favor of Olodumare! Show me how to rise in the glory of my destiny! Let success be mines! Good health is mine! Financial blessing in abundance is mine! Happiness is mine! Good children is mine! Good character is mine! Patience is mine! Love is mine! Peace is mine! Success is mine!

Orinmilla, Akoda and Aseda thank you so much for all that you did, do and is still doing!

Bless my prayers today, bring sweetness and positive direction into my life, and don't allow any energy to steal my destiny my gifts or my virtue! Don't allow them to steal what I have worked for or even what was given to me or what I am about to receive! Give me that protection or the ingredients for that protection!

Ase Olodumare! AseOrisa!

EGBE (HEAVENLY FAMILY)

Greetings Egbe my heavenly family!

I am aware of your support of me here in the physical realm!

I give you thanks for doing the required sacrifices for me to have physical life at this time!

Egbe thank you ooh! Support me in my life!

Do not affect me in a negative way!

Don't put obstacles in my way! Let me have a good physical spouse!

Do not interfere negatively in my relationships, but you may guide me to one, align my positive growth and development!

Let me get married let me have children! Support me to have a good life!

Communicate with me so that I can make sweet offerings to you!

My heavenly family must support me!

I honor you I respect you!

Egbe life in the physical form is good!

I am very happy and successful in the physical!

Egbe support me to be better, let me be known among the successful, abundant, prosperous, flourishing, fruitful, people here on earth!

Egbe do not let me be disgraced!

Egbe do not let any entity take advantage of me!

Egbe help me and give me good fortune!

Egbe let me have good house, good relationships, goo children, good lifestyle, abundance of wealth, courage, good health, protection from dangers seen and unseen, blessing of great things here on earth!

My egbe will not disrupt my life! My Egbe will support my life and the life of my spouse and the life of my children!

Egbe support my desires, let me live a fulfilling life on earth, long happy life is what I desire!

Ase Olodumare! Ase Olodumare! Ase Olodumare!

ANCESTORS

Divine ancestors I call on you to come and support your child of this moment, come and bring me elevation! Remove the chains of stagnation! Remove the blockages in my path!

Dissolve the weapons of my enemies!

Dismiss the sadness from my way bring healing as I call on you today! Speak to me I am your child a part of your DNA, assist me on this journey to self!

The journey to truth the journey to our god almighty!

I know there are many ways to do things but please show me the easiest way! I know you toiled in this physical plain, to make the way for me to come! I am so grateful for your works! Reveal your wisdom onto me!

Activate me to become the person I am to be! Open my eyes to see what needs to be seen!

Open my ears to hear the speech! Open my mind to understanding!

Open my nose to smell the smell! Open my mouth to speak the truth and things that are beneficial!

My ancestors come to me, come and reveal thyself to me! Come and bring healing to my body!

Come and shine light onto my path come and resurrect the sleeping information lying dormant in my soul!

Ancestors from before my slavery and bondage of the mind, even those from recent times, come and teach your pickney today! Do not harm me ancestors!

Ancestors come only if you are coming to assist me to become a better person, to ascend my prayers to god!

Speak to me in visions and dreams, speak to me in my ears, and speak to me in my eyesight! Direct me to being the greatest version of myself show me how to work magic teach me how to heal! Show me how to defend myself, but still protect me from those that stand against me!

I call you from the depths of my being today, come and see me!

Ase Olodumare! Ase Olodumare! Ase Olodumare!

TO REMOVE MISFORTUNE

No negative event will occur in my life! I cleanse my space my aura and my path of all undesirable events! By the power and authority that I stand with I command misfortune assigned to myself or my amicable family members or directed to peaceful members of my temple to become powerless!

Any negative curse assigned to my name I command you to go back to the sender!

All unfortunate events must pass me by! Whoever or whatever sent you command you to go away!

Bad luck go away! Disaster remove yourself away from me! Loss and tragedy be gone sorrow and pain be gone!

Broken days, suffering, loneliness, heart break, mishap, accident, incident, trouble, misery, burden, failure, sickness, ill health, calamity, set back, difficulty, disappointment, loss, inconvenience, bad news, distress, unpleasant experiences, weakness, drought, anxiety, poverty, evil, disaster, mischief, death, stagnation, depression, doubtfulness, gloominess, grief, agony, scattered feeling, doom, nastiness, hatred, unfairness, be gone!

You have no path in my life! I rebuke you! You have no power here! You are powerless there is no room for you in my presence! if someone sent your bitterness to me I tell you go back to your sender and reside there! In the name of Olodumare and all my spirit guides retreat to where you came from and reside there!

All my powerful ancestors stand with me against any misfortune that is trying to enter! Diminish it and make it powerless in my life!

My Ori rejects anything that is meant to destroy me!

My Ori rejects anything sent by my enemies! My god clothed me with powerful armor so no evil can penetrate! Be gone all attacks against me go and stay with the ones who sent you!

Ase Olodumare! Ase Olodumare! Ase Olodumare!

PEACE

Spirit is of peace welcome, come and fill my life fill my vessel fill my home! Fill the lives of my family let there be peace in my soul and peace in this world!

Let my day be peaceful and calm and harmonious!

Inner peace come and fill me up let me feel your relaxing mood! Peace resides in my heart and mind!

I am now filled with contentment, nothing shall shift my balance today!

Peace aligns me with my spirit self, I am one with peace, peace be one with me!

Peace resides in my aura, let me be able to bring peace in any situation!

spirit of peace invite into my life your friends of faith, joy, love happiness, light, understanding, compassion, comfort, healing, optimism, balance, trust and eternal grace!

Let me have peace in my life, peace I welcome you to stay!

Keep changing me into what god desires me to be to have a character that is good and nobble!

Let me shear this peace with others do not let my journey be in vane I must have peace daily, just as I have life let me have peace and peace bring me your gifts!

Ase Olodumare! Ase Olodumare! Ase Olodumare!

PRAYER TO A TREE

Tree full of life I give thanks for your magnificence, a tree ha roots penetrating deep into the earth and branches sprouting up to the heavens, arms going to each cardinal point.

A home to what crawls on the ground and what flies in the air what a place to come for help, where so many healing spirits reside. The tree must know what's above and below and uses both to grow.

A tree absorbs and turns one type of energy into another to benefit nature, therefore I ask the permission of this tree, to absorb my sorrow and pain, me weakness, my fears, my sadness my failures and change it into something good.

Spirit of the tree from the root to the top hear my call for help, for physical and spiritual nourishment and transformation.

I affirm you will do only positive things for me, like bring healing and renewal prosperous growth and development..

Now you may add your personal Iwori for assistance from nature

PRAYER BEFORE MEALS

Thank you god and goddess for this meal,

as I am about to eat, I affirm that any negative energy from this food become harmless now!

I affirm that from the farmer to the hands that prepared this meal be blessed!

That as I consume this meal I am nourished, revitalized, and healthy! I will always have good clean food to eat, and clean beverages to drink to refuel my body!

I place a small morsel on the side in appreciation to creation, the earth, and my divine ancestors, as I remember you I know you will continue to provide for me.

This meal will bring healing to all that eat of it!

As this food be blessed let this day be blessed, and may those without food also be blessed with a meal!

Ase Olodumare! Ase Olodumare! Ase Olodumare!

PRAYER FOR FEEDING FISHES

Come fishes come and enjoy and feast on this offering I bring to you!

As I feed you, listen to my request!

Release me of my debts, send money flowing toward me to clear off my debts!

It's a blessing I seek, fishes you represent fertility, good luck, intelligence, transformation, abundance, and I call on the owner of the fishes to come and witness my plight for help!

I am here to receive your gifts, as I come bearing gifts of food, deliver me from drought in my life!

Let me have abundance in my life!

Let me have joy, love, happiness and peace, education and elevation!

I ask for good job in my life!

Security wherever I go, protection wherever I thread!

Help me to understand when nature speaks!

Deliver me from wicked and evil! Raise my head above troubled waters!

Help me to find my path in life! Bless the offspring of my body with abundance of love and peace!

Protect our mental physical and spiritual health!

Keep me moving toward the glory of God!

Keep me in the grace of the ever flowing fountain!

Multiply my blessings and my support!

Let me always have shelter and clothes, let me always have mobility!

Let me always have victory! Let me leave here in a better situation than the one I came in!

I am leaving my burdens at the river side, let all the burdens be washed away, don't let it bring harm to anyone! Don't let it return onto me, but let it be lost to no return!

I shake off all that has been holding me back I command the burdens to leave and flow away! Flow away and Sale away to no return!

I thank you fishes for the opportunity to pour my problems at your space, thanks for cleaning up my life may we be forever blessed!

Ase Olodumare! Ase Olodumare! Ase Olodumare!

PRAYER TO THE ELEMENTS
Earth, wind, fire, water, spirit

Earth

The earth is abundant, the earth is rich, the earth is fertile, the earth is a beautiful paradise a home to all that resides in it, a free giving life sustaining embodiment of love, the element of the earth will not work against me, the element of the earth will always work in my favor, earth will always protect me heal me, restore me and uplift me the earth is here to assist me so the earth will not work against me.

The earth is ever regenerating sending healing crystals to assist me, the earth is a blessing to mankind the earth feeds me, this is why I feed the earth, and the earth multiplies one grain into many plants and grains and the earth multiplies my success just as it multiplies grains yielding bountiful harvest, wisdom, knowledge and wealth. The earth is the home of the physical the earth is the material that gives form and life to the physical. I give praise to the earth, I request the support of the earth in all my endeavors, because I am a child of the earth!

Wind

The wind is always present the element of wind will support me in my life, the wind has supported me from the first breath of life and will continue to work in my favor, wind must not work against me, wind will always sustain my life, the energy of the wind will not bring me destruction. The wind will give me oxygen, the wind will blow away my worries, and the wind will always blow my blessings to me to receive, I sweeten the air with fragrant incense and perfume, I respect the power of the wind, the winds of heaven and the winds of earth supports me, the wind makes me cool and not cold. Help me to understand the messages in the wind, the wind bring me protection, good health wealth wisdom knowledge understanding and wealth the wind extends my life, and the element of the wind takes care of me, because I am a child of the wind.

Fire

I give praise and thanks to the element of fire, I give thanks for your light and warmth. Fire will not work against me as I am a child of the fire. Fire supports my needs and wants fire purifies, it reflects passion the courageous heart that fights, the strength to overcome. Fire light my way but do not burn me, fire give me encouragement to attain my goals, fire removes negativity from affecting me, fire uses its positive side with me, I ask that you bless my efforts and keep me safe. I live my life as the element of fire keeps fueling me and give me assistance of wisdom knowledge protection health keeping the flame within me burning bright and elevating me with flaming success.

Water

Water I give thanks for your sustenance of life, water will not work against me because I am a child of the waters, water you cleanse me daily you hydrate the world, refresh me always thanking you for always quenching my thirst. The element of water is found in what lives, water will continue to give me life and abundance, you are essential you are a great supporter of life, a great protector, a fine defender, the one who keeps me cool, water is life, water is prosperity, water is memory, water gives me abundance, replenish my life, refresh my memory, restore my health, fertilize my finances, precious water give me abundance of protection, wisdom, creativity, knowledge positive growth and development. Thanks to the element of water.

Spirit

Giving honor to the element of spirit, as I am a spirit being having a physical experience spirit of god supports me, spirit will always work in my favor and see me through my successful journey. Spirit ensures I have a joyous fulfilling successful life, as spirit communicates with me always assisting me leading me to good places good people and the correct decisions that creates the best version of myself, divine spirit is always with me, the spirit of alinement fixes my path and ensures that I am divinely aligned to fulfilling my purpose and receiving my birthright of happy successful physical life in this realm.

Giving praise and thanks to Olodumare and for the very elements that sustains our life, earth, wind, fire, water, and spirit, east, west, north and south, heaven and earth, continue to bless me and elevate me I affirm that you all will continue to give answers to my calls.

Ase Ase Ase

PRAYER FOR PROTECTION AND DELIVERANCE FROM A VERY EVIL ENEMY

It is I (state your Name) calling on Olodumare and all my spirit guides at this time come forward and protect me from all dangers and wickedness arise and come to bring me victory in my battles.

I call on you spirit of God come and defend me.

Spirit of goddess come and defend me.

Spirit of my ancestors come and defend me.

Spirit of truth come and defend me.

Spirit of justice come and defend me.

Spirit of the crossroad come and defend me.

Spirit of iron come and defend me.

Spirit of direction come and defend me.

Spirit of the river come and defend me.

Spirit of the sun come and defend me.

Spirit of the moon come and defend me.

Spirit of the wind come and defend me.

Spirit of the rain and waters come and defend me.

Spirit of lightning and thunder come and defend me.

Spirit of fire come and defend me.

Spirit of the earth come and defend me.

Spirit of heaven and heavenly family come and defend me.

Spirit of herbs and nature come and defend me.

Spirit of wealth come and defend me.

Spirit of peace come and defend me.

Spirit of wisdom come and defend me.

Spirit of health come and defend me.

Spirit who sees all and knows all come and defend me.

Spirit of war come and defend me.

Spirit of victory come and defend me.

Spirit of the east come and defend me.

Spirit of the west come and defend me.

Spirit of the north come and defend me

Spirit of the south come and defend me.

Spirit of my body come and defend me.

Spirit of creation come and defend me.

Spirit of my head spirit of my home I call on you all to arise to my defense bring who is needed on this army to defend me against those who has risen up against me.

In the name of Olodumare, Ori, Egbe,Imale,Orisa,Ancestors and all my spirit guides I rebuke all evil and wickedness I rebuke you. Those who sent you to destroy I command you to go back to the sender and devour them for the have risen against me without just cause they are trying to make my path different from what the creator has made for me therefore they that try to make my path slippery and dark let that be their destiny. For no negativity can affect me go back to them and live there and make yourself as a torn in their flesh that they find no peace until they stop speaking evil and doing evil. Let the poison that the wicked has sent let them inherit it today. Let them have it when the sun rises, let them have it in the midday heat, let them have it in the cool of night, while they sleep and while they wake give onto them their iniquities that they sent. Attach yourself to their life suck and feed on them just like they sent you to cause me harm let them destroy their own self. Let the pain they sent be their daily experience let them remember all the wickedness they do without just cause let them realize all they wanted people to go through it is that that they are going through and that it is they themselves that made their own path dark and slippery. I rebuke every attack against my life and my family life I rebuke all vibrations of hate and stagnation. I rebuke all attacks on my businesses.

Those who wat to see me fall they will fall.

Those who want to see me fail they will fail.

Those who want to see me die they will die.

They who use spirits of evil against the innocent must be brought to shame.

Expose them and shame them let them reap the hate they planted and fall into the very grave they digging for the innocent. Make haste and go back and make residence with those who sent you.

Heavenly spirits deliver me from all sorrows, come and defend me and all that is mine, come and strengthen me and rise me above my enemies today make a wall around me that the enemy cannot breach, let those who ill speak me choke on their lies, let me live my life of abundance happiness and peace, let all attacks from the enemies be null and void against my camp. Clear my path from all evil deliver me today.

Ase Olodumare, Ase Olodumare, Ase Olodumare.

BASIC ITEMS USED TO OFFER TO ORISA AND WHY IT'S USED

Some of these things can be used to specific Orisa as long as you know their taboo, and use cowrie, obi or whichever divination system you use to communicate with the energies to ensure the Orisa or Imale wants that item at that time ti bring about positive growth and development for yourself, your family and your community.

Using genie pepper (ataare) (pepper of blessings) by chewing a few seeds before praying or making an offering, is said to enhance the power of your Ase or spoken word.

- Water (Yoruba name Omi)
- Water can be used to cleanse and bring clarity
- To give life
- To Revitilize
- Has memory
- Find its way around any obstacle
- Brings calmness
- It sustains etc.

Rum (Yoruba name Oti)
- Brings victory

- Joyfulness
- Reasons to celebrate
- Different brands and flavors will be used for different reasons
- That shame won't come to your name

Honey (Yoruba name Oyin)

- Sweetness
- Long life
- Prosperity
- Peace, love

Oil (Yoruba name Epo)

- For things to run smooth and effortlessly in your life and make your pathway smooth
- Oil rises above
- Brings wealth
- Soothing and lubrication to a situation

Red palm oil (Yoruba name Epo pupa)

- To protect
- To calm
- Brings good health
- To calm situations
- To lubricate and bring victory

Wine

- Celebration
- Sweetness
- Victory
- Cleansing
- Happiness

Light or fire

- To purify to sanctify
- To open and clear a pathway
- To illuminate ones way
- To make pure and holy

Molasses

- Strength
- Richness

Money (Yoruba name Owo)

- For richness
- For wealth
- To pay for something

Salt (Yoruba name Iyo)

- To remove negativity
- To cleanse and purify
- To bring victory and blessings

Kola nut (Yoruba name Obi)

- Brings greatness
- Prosperity
- Can prevent loss
- Brings victory and blessings

Bitter kola nut (Yoruba name Orogbo)

- To find spouse
- To have children
- To overcome situation

KEISHA EFUNTOLA TEMIDAYO

Keisha is a vibrant tapestry of creative expression, woven from the rich cultural threads of her island home, Trinidad and Tobago.

A visual and performing artist, her very essence pulses with the rhythms of song and dance. As a singer-songwriter, she weaves melodic spells that transport the soul. With fluid grace, she moves across the stage, choreographing movements that tell stories of joy and wonder.

Beyond the stage, her deft hands craft beautiful beaded jewelry, each piece a unique work of art. And her artistic vision manifests in diverse media - painting, sculpture, poetry. Every creation an extension of her vibrant, multifaceted self.

Martina is a conduit of abundance, sharing freely the gifts that flow through her - joy, love, knowledge, peace, happiness, and positivity. Her art is her imprint on the world, a testament to the power of self-expression and the transformative beauty that arises when we embrace all the wondrous parts that make us whole.

https://www.facebook.com/martina.kadoo

Made in the USA
Monee, IL
28 July 2024